Barry Rowe

CAR
BOOK

How a car is made
from the design board to the transporter

COLLINS COLOUR CUBS

The first petrol-driven motor cars were made before the year 1900. Some of these early cars still survive in transport museums or in private collections and are occasionally brought out for an airing at events such as the London to Brighton Old Crocks Run. Compared with present day cars, they look rather strange as they go chugging and banging along.

These old cars were very expensive to build. Every single part had to be made by hand. This took a long time and, because of this, cost a great deal of money. In these early days, cars were a luxury which only the very rich could afford. Some people regarded them as a passing fashion. Many were convinced they would never replace the horse.

But more and more people wanted motor cars.
Men began to think of ways to manufacture them
that would be quicker
and cheaper.

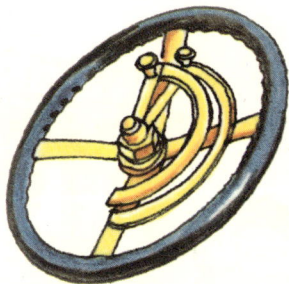

The first step in this direction
was to have other people
make the parts which were
then fitted together by the
manufacturers
who made the
complete car.

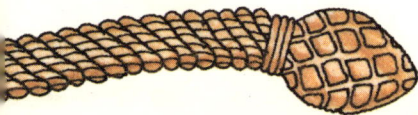

Henry Ford, an American, developed the idea of the assembly line. Men brought the parts to the car. Other men fitted each part on to the car, then moved on to another car. This cut down the manufacturing time and cost. Henry Ford's Model T car was the first really popular car.

As soon as one line of cars was completed, the cars were driven out of the workshop and another line of cars to be assembled took their place.

Nowadays, the cars in the factories come to the men on a moving track. This improvement on the old method means that cars can be built in greater numbers and much more quickly.

The car industry now employs thousands of people. Apart from those who actually build the cars, there are thousands busy turning out parts.

The tracks on which the cars move along are controlled by a computer. The man at the computer can see at a glance just what is happening on all the tracks. The computer tells him if they are working properly.

When a new model of a car is planned, it starts life as a drawing on a drawing-board.

The designers have to think of every aspect of the car, even to the position of the ashtrays. New engines are developed to give smoother running. The engineers try to make sure that the new engines will use less petrol. Particular attention is paid to the suspension unit by the designers.

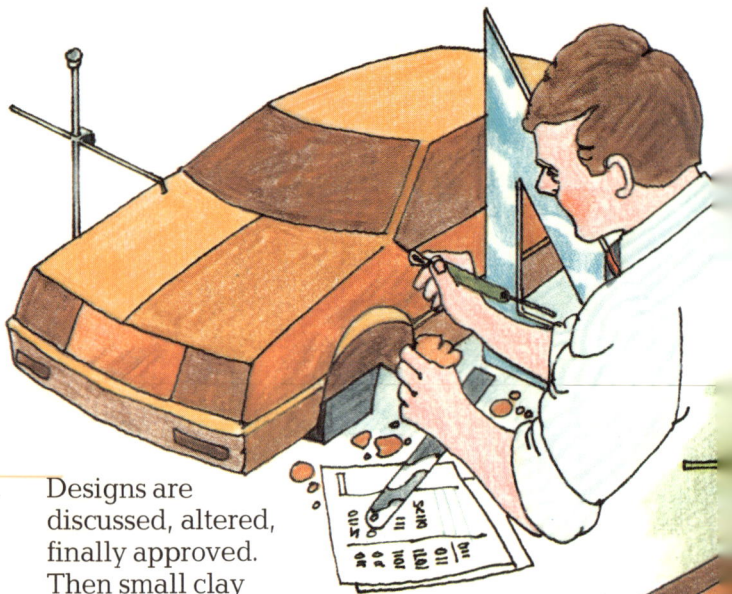

Designs are
discussed, altered,
finally approved.
Then small clay
models are made.
These look exactly like a
car. They even have
windows and
wheels
fitted.

When the shape of the new car is agreed from the clay models, the next stage is to make a full-sized mock-up of the car-to-be. This is constructed of clay and wood. It is then painted to look like a real car. This stage of the work is kept very secret.

The first models, called prototypes, are built by hand. The shape is tested in a wind tunnel to ensure that the new car will run smoothly with the minimum of wind resistance.

The proto-
types then
undergo
practical tests
in real life con-
ditions. They
are driven over
thousands of miles
on the worst roads of
different countries.
Alterations are made
and parts changed in
accordance with the
lessons learned from the
very severe trials.

The new car has now reached the stage of being ready to go into mass-production. The bodies are pressed out of sheets of steel. The steel has previously been cut out into shapes.

The sheets of steel are fed into giant presses. They come out as doors, wings, roofs and other car parts. They are then ready for the next stage which is called welding.

All the pressed steel parts are put together. The welders fuse these parts together using very hot flames that melt the steel. The welders wear dark shields over their heads and eyes.

These protect them from sparks and the bright flame. These flames reach a temperature of between 8,000 and 10,000 degrees centigrade. Once the parts are welded together, they are smoothed down with grinding wheels.

The next process is to clean all the grease off the body shell. Then the car is taken for a bath. An overhead track passes it through a tank filled with rust-proofing liquid.

The rust-proofing process is very thorough. Each car body is lowered into the tank and then turned over and over to ensure that the car will be protected against rusting.

The car body comes out
of the rust-proofing tank a sad
dull colour like chocolate
that has been kept too
long in a drawer.

To remedy this, the cars go on to the paint track. The bodies are painted by men using spray guns and wearing protective masks against the paint fumes. Once the finished colour has been applied, the cars go into ovens where the paint is baked hard.

At the end of the paint track, the car bodies are scanned by electronic eyes. If no fault is found, the bodies are lifted by automatic arms on to an overhead track. They are now on their way to the assembly lines.

A great many of the parts that go to make up a motor car are made in different factories. Some factories make car wheels, others make tyres, door locks, windows, handles, instruments, lights and brakes. These are all brought to the factory of the car manufacturer by large lorries.

The car bodies are now placed on a slow-moving track which is called the trim line. Here, all the parts are fitted. Some men fit the lights, others fit the windows. The man in the picture is putting on the lock handle.

At the end of the trim line, all the parts have been fitted to the car. Quality control checks are then carried out by skilled inspectors.

A second moving track runs alongside the trim line and on this one, groups of men are busy, fitting the sub frame and the engine. They are also responsible for the brakes and other components on the bottom side of the car. At this point, the car is nearing completion. The final touches will be put to it during the next stage which is when the two parts of the car are lifted on to the finishing track.

The finishing track travels above floor level. This enables men to work underneath and inside the cars.

The top and bottom of the car are finally bolted
together. The controls are connected to the engine.
The wheels are put on with the tyres already blown up.

Now the petrol tank is filled; oil is put in the gear-box and water in the radiator.

Next, the car is started up and driven on to a rolling road. The gears are tested at speed and the car is then driven down to try out the brakes. Any faults that show up are put right. These tests are repeated over and over again until the inspectors are satisfied.

Every car manufacturer has to think a great deal about the very important question of safety on the road. He knows only too well that crashes do happen; and it is important for him to find out how his new model will stand up to a crash.

The safety tests carried out on each new model are very tough and severe. Life-sized dummies are used to represent driver and passenger, and the car is crashed at high speed. From these crashes, the experts work out what is likely to happen to the car and its passengers in a real life accident.

The tests have all been carried out and the finished cars are ready to leave the factory. You may have seen the huge transporter lorries loaded with cars.

Other cars are loaded on to special car-carrying trains. Most factories employ a car delivery driver whose job is to deliver a single car.

Most of the cars that are manufactured in the factories are for export, which means that they are sold abroad.

If you were to watch these export cars being loaded into the ships that are specially adapted for carrying them, you would notice many differences from your own car. The steering wheel might be on the opposite side. The headlights are sometimes different. For countries with lots of sunshine, the windows may be tinted.

Every car that you see, new and gleaming, in the car showroom among the potted plants, has been given a very thorough pre-delivery check by the skilled garage mechanics.

The sport of International Rally Driving is something more than a sport to many of the big motor companies. A successful car means valuable publicity and more cars sold in the showroom. So the companies employ the best drivers from all over the world.

The modern motor car has come a long way from
those early hand-made models that only people
with lots of money could afford. Nowadays, mass-
production means that more and more people can
afford to run a car. This has changed the whole
face of the countryside as new motorways have
been built to deal with the flood of cars. Motorway
cafés have appeared to cater for the needs of
travellers. Motels have been built where you can
sleep overnight.

A whole new way of life has been brought about
by the car. So next time you wave to a veteran
car, remember, you are waving to your own car's
great-great-great grandfather which was about to
change the world.

TEXT BY EDWARD BOYD

Illustrations Copyright © 1978 Barry Rowe
Text Copyright © 1978 Wm. Collins Sons & Co. Ltd.
ISBN 0 00 123258 4
Printed in Great Britain